Northumberland

Stuart Miller

COUNTRYSIDE BOOKS
NEWBURY BERKSHIRE

First Published 2007
© Stuart Miller, 2007

All rights reserved. No reproduction
permitted without the prior permission
of the publisher:

COUNTRYSIDE BOOKS
3 Catherine Road
Newbury, Berkshire

To view our complete range of books,
please visit us at
www.countrysidebooks.co.uk

ISBN 978 1 84674 021 3

Photographs by the author

*Cover picture of Craster
supplied by Pictures of Britain (Michael Durman)*

Designed by Peter Davies, Nautilus Design
Maps by Gelder Design & Mapping

Produced through MRM Associates Ltd, Reading
Typeset by CJWT Solutions, St Helens
Printed by Cambridge University Press

Contents

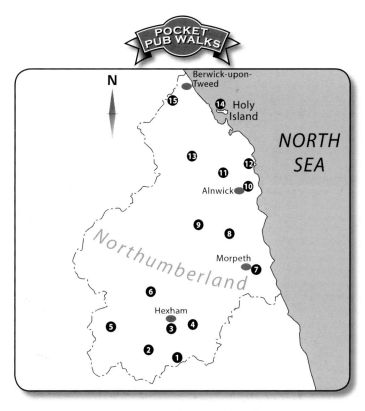

POCKET PUB WALKS

N

Berwick-upon-Tweed

⑮

⑭ Holy Island

NORTH SEA

⑬

⑪ ⑫

Alnwick ⑩

Northumberland

⑨ ⑧

Morpeth ⑦

⑥

Hexham

⑤ ③ ④

② ①

Area map showing location of the walks

Introduction

Northumberland is the northernmost county of England, indeed a large area of it is further north than parts of Scotland, and in extent, 2,000 square miles, it is exceeded only by Yorkshire. This is a county with a beautiful and varied landscape. It has attracted famous artists and film producers alike. On celluloid Henry II and Becket strolled Northumberland's 'Lordly Strand', Robin Hood fought opponents by the sycamore on the Roman Wall and Harry Potter has flown in the skies above Alnwick Castle. Certainly, the landscape artist J.M.W. Turner was attracted to Northumberland on numerous occasions. Yet the county also played a vital part in the industrial development of Britain, and on the walks in this book you will encounter evidence of this in the most unlikely places, as well as some of the most beautiful and dramatic scenery to be found in England.

Hadrian's remarkable wall was the limit of Roman jurisdiction in this island for 250 years. In Saxon times Northumberland was a substantial part of the ancient kingdom of Northumbria which extended south to the Midlands and north into the Lothians. Then, and after the Norman Conquest, it was governed by a series of earls endowed with near regal authority but who frequently clashed with the Crown. Of course, the ever-present threat of war with Scotland and ongoing border reiving necessitated such devolution of authority. The county is therefore rich in the castles and fortified houses of the gentry and nobility, who are frequently commemorated in the inn names of Northumberland. However, it was also of key significance in the story of Christianity in England. St Paulinus converted thousands of Northumbrians near Wooler, and Lindisfarne, or Holy Island, was the home of the iconic St Cuthbert.

One of Northumberland's greatest qualities is freedom from the pressures of our fast moving modern world. It is one of the least densely populated areas in Britain. No longer can you see the white sails of Newcastle shipping from the top of the Cheviot as Defoe claimed, but the air is still clear and it is the English county with the least light pollution. In 2006 it was declared to be the highest ranking English county in a league table of 'tranquillity'. Not surprisingly it attracts visitors back again and again.

This selection of rambles and inns will give you a good flavour of the 'Secret Kingdom'. The circular routes range from 3 to 6 miles in length and each begins and ends at an excellent Northumberland hostelry. Details of opening times, food and drink are given, and there is also a note on other places of interest in the area. Enjoy...

Stuart Miller

Publisher's Note

We hope that you obtain considerable enjoyment from this book; great care has been taken in its preparation. However, changes of landlord and actual closures are sadly not uncommon. Likewise, although at the time of publication all routes followed public rights of way or permitted paths, diversion orders can be made and permissions withdrawn.

We cannot, of course, be held responsible for such diversion orders and any inaccuracies in the text which result from these or any other changes to the routes nor any damage which might result from walkers trespassing on private property. We are anxious though that all details covering the walks are kept up to date and would therefore welcome information from readers which would be relevant to future editions.

The simple sketch maps that accompany the walks in this book are based on notes made by the author whilst checking out the routes on the ground. However, for the benefit of a proper map, we do recommend that you purchase the relevant Ordnance Survey sheet covering your walk. The Ordnance Survey maps are widely available, especially through booksellers and local newsagents.

1 Blanchland

The Lord Crewe Arms

Blanchland is a delightful stone-built model village on the banks of the River Derwent, clustered round the church and nestled within woodland and moors. The name is derived from the white robes of the monks of the Premonstratensian abbey, which was founded in 1175 and dissolved in 1539. The village layout is based on the monastic plan and the church comprises the former chancel, crossing and north transept of the abbey church. This area was also noteworthy for the prevalence

Distance – 3½ miles.

OS Explorer 307 Consett and the Derwent Reservoir.
GR 965505.
There are a couple of minor slopes and some brief road walking. This is an easy walk.

Starting point The Lord Crewe Arms in Blanchland.

How to get there Blanchland is on the B6306, which links with the A69 at Hexham in the north and via the B6278 with Consett in the east and the A689 to Alston in the south. The Lord Crewe Arms is in the centre of the village. You can park in front of the pub or in the main car park in the village centre.

of lead and fluorspar mining which has left very visible marks on the fells around and the remains of structures built for the purpose. Most of this walk is over pastureland with attractive views along the Derwent valley. The final section is along the riverbank and a gentle bridleway stroll.

THE PUB The mostly Georgian **Lord Crewe Arms** was once the lodge of the Abbot of Blanchland and the abbey guesthouse. The attractive garden was the cloisters. The bar is in a stone barrel-vaulted former storeroom. The Hilyard Room, the lounge, with its huge fireplace was a room used by the monks for curing and storing bacon. The south wall of the monastic church survives as the boundary between the inn garden and the abbey churchyard. The inn is haunted by the ghost of Dorothy Forster, niece of Lord Crewe, the Bishop of Durham, who rode in disguise to Newgate Prison to rescue her brother Tom, imprisoned for his part in the Jacobite rising of 1715. The main beers are Black Sheep, Boddington's and John Smith's. There is an excellent range of bar meals available, and at very reasonable prices. Lord Crewe himself is unwittingly included as sponsor of an appetising tossed salad alongside Cumberland sausage with black pudding, breast of chicken with mango sauce, rump steak and many other dishes. There is a children's selection as well and a children's room next to the bar. Dogs are welcome.

Open from 11 am to 11 pm. Coffees are available from 10 am to 12 pm. Bar lunches are served from 12 pm to 2 pm, then afternoon teas from 2.30 pm to 5.30 pm, bar meals from 7 pm to 9 pm and dinner in the restaurant from 7 pm to 9.15 pm.
☎ *01434 675251; website: www.LordCreweArms.com*

1 From the **Lord Crewe Arms** turn right and walk up to the main car park. Past the entrance to the car park turn left up the walled track towards **Cote House** (signed confusingly to **Coat House**).

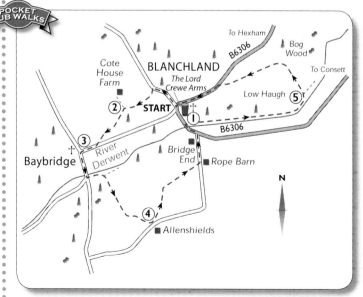

The River Derwent at Baybridge.

2. Where the track turns right towards the farmhouse, turn left through a waymarked gate. Walk to the opposite corner of the small field and cross a ladder stile. Bear half-left down the hillside – with a good view up the valley – to cross another ladder stile onto a road.

3. Turn right on the road and walk into the hamlet of **Baybridge**. Cross the **River Derwent** and enter County Durham by means of the stone bridge. Past a road signed back towards **Baybridge** and **Blanchland**, turn left onto a footpath by a gate. You cross a stream after a few yards. Turn right and go uphill through woods to reach a kissing gate. Go through this gate and then bear half-right across the field and follow the fence up to the right corner. When you reach the top, turn left through a gateway and follow the track through another gate to the farm of **Allenshields** where you go through a series of metal gates in the farmyard.

[4] Beyond the farmyard bear left across a field to a ladder stile. Cross the stile and then follow the right field edge. Cross another ladder stile and a small stone slab bridge and then bear left over the field to exit by means of a gate near a house called **Rope Barn**. Turn left along the lane and then turn left at a T-junction to re-enter Northumberland and cross **Blanchland Bridge**. Turn back along the side of the bridge, walking between it and a stone building to reach a path along the banks of the **Derwent**. Follow the path, crossing two ladder stiles within a couple of yards of each other.

[5] At a three-way signpost turn left along the bridleway to **Blanchland**. Follow a track, ignoring paths intersecting from the right, which rises and bends sharp left. You reach a road, which you cross and turn left, walking down a raised footway, back into **Blanchland**.

Place of interest nearby

The **Allenheads Heritage Centre** is in the highest village in England in the North Pennines 17 miles south-west of Hexham on the B6295. It describes the fascinating past and present of a small lead-mining village. Former mine buildings house interpretative displays, a blacksmith's shop of the time, a restored Armstrong pumping engine from nearby workings and a coffee shop (closed Mondays). Behind the centre is a nature trail with some excellent walks.

☎ 01434 685395

2 Allendale Town

The King's Head

Allendale Town stands amidst spectacular scenery in the North Pennines, at the geographical centre of Britain. It is famous for the Baal Fire celebration on New Year's Eve when 'guysers' dress up and blacken their faces to carry blazing tar barrels round the town on their heads. Look out for Isaac's Well (1849) at the start of this walk. Isaac Holden was a well-known Methodist, a former lead-miner turned itinerant tea seller who was popular because of his good works for the Allendale community. There is a circular walk of 36 miles known as Isaac's Tea Trail – a little too long for our purposes though! The outward section of this walk is across fields and then on a quiet road with excellent views across Allendale. The return section is delightful as you walk along the valley of the bubbling River East Allen on clear waymarked paths.

THE PUB The **King's Head** and the Golden Lion were originally one big coaching inn, with stables and outhouses at the rear. The King's Head is more than 300 years old – and the stone floors and beams are original. With its dark, intimate interior and real fire it exudes character. Its friendly staff contribute to the sense that this is a genuine village 'local'. The main beers are Jenning's (Cumberland Bitter), Marston's Pedigree and Banks's Original Bitter. A good range of sandwiches and large filled rolls is available as well as reasonably priced wholesome meals of good quality – the usual selection of steak, gammon, chicken, scampi, haddock and roast beef. There is also accommodation.

Opening times are 11 am to 11 pm. Food is served between 12 noon and 2.30 pm and 6.30 pm and 9 pm.
☎ *01434 683681*

Distance – 6 miles or 4 miles.

OS Explorer OL43 Hadrian's Wall, Haltwhistle and Hexham. GR 837559.
There are two slopes to ascend – one at the start and a second (stepped) towards the end of the walk. There are numerous stiles, but often beside gates. Always leave gates as you find them.

Starting point The King's Head in Allendale Town.

How to get there *Allendale Town is on the B6295 which links the A686 and the A689, 11 miles to the south-west of Hexham. The King's Head is on the north edge of the market place and you can park by the side of the pub.*

Northumberland

1 From the **Kings Head**, walk down with the Co-op to the left and cross the road beside Lloyds Bank. In the wall opposite is **Isaac's Well** (also known as the Bobbies' Well because it stands outside the former police station). Go up the little flight of steps next to it. Walk up the path between council houses and a children's playground. Cross the road to the **Finney Hill Green** signpost. Walk up a short enclosed path to go through a gap into the field. From here you bear right and walk up a slope over a series of fields crossing several waymarked stiles. The first is in the right hand wall; the second in the top, facing wall (beneath a tree); and the third in the wall to the right (with a gap next to the stile). Cross over the middle of the next field to a stile in a small fenced enclosure. Cross a private drive and then cross a wooden stile. Continue with a wall to your right to cross a ladder stile (with a gap next to it). Walk on with the wall to your right to the corner

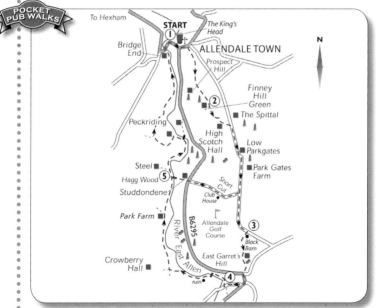

View up the Allen from near Sinderhope.

and then on to a stone stile. **Finney Hill Farm** is on the left but you cross the stile onto the drive of **Finney Hill Green Farm**.

2 Turn right along the drive. Cross a stile by two gates and enter the field. Bear left towards **High Scotch Hall**. Cross a stone stile, then follow the field wall round to the left, crossing a stone stile on the left into a lane. Turn right and walk between the farm buildings to exit onto a road. Turn right and follow this, passing a lane on your right to the golf course. *(You could shorten this walk to 4 miles by going down this very pleasant lane. Cross a road and descend a winding track from Studdondene Farm to reach a metal bridge. Cross this and then cross the stile. Turn right and follow the route from the end of Point 4.)* After the road bends between **Holms Hill** and **Green Hill** go through a wicket gate on the right (signed **Sinderhope**) near a black barn.

3 Walk between walls for a few yards, then turn left and walk downhill past a copse on the left. Continue round to the right and cross a wooden stile. Descend over pasture to a stile to the right

of some Scots pine trees near **East Garret's Hill Farm**. Cross the stile and then the large field diagonally to the right corner and exit onto the B6295 at **Sinderhope**. Cross **Sinderhope Bridge**, then turn right along a lane. At a sign to **Crowberry Hall** on the right, go through a kissing gate.

4 Descend on the path alongside the **River East Allen** to go through another kissing gate and walk on to cross a footbridge to the left. Turn right at the end of this and walk towards a ruined farm. Cross a stone block stile behind it. From here follow the river on a clear, maintained, waymarked path. It is diverted slightly in a meadow before a small patch of woodland. Then continue from a four-fingered signpost past **Park Farm** and the end of a metal bridge over the **East Allen**. *(The 4-mile version of this walk brings you across this bridge from the east side)*.

5 Continue past a second footbridge over the **East Allen** then ascend a flight of steps past a house on the right. Exit into a field through a wicket gate. Bear right up the slope to the right and cross a stile on the right. Turn right to cross a ladder stile. Follow the waymarks again with the river now far below you. You go through a white gate onto a road near restored buildings at **Bridge End**. Follow the road to the bridge, then cross over and walk back into **Allendale**.

Place of interest nearby

The **North of England Lead Mining Museum** is at Killhope, near the junction of the B6295 and the A689. Attractions include guided tours, hands-on activities, a mineral exhibition, a working 10-metre Armstrong waterwheel and the last pure red squirrel colony in County Durham. There is also a café and a shop.
☎ 01388 537505; website: www.durham.gov.uk/killhope

The Dipton Mill Inn

Diptonmill is a hamlet on the Dipton Burn, a tributary of the Devil's Water. This very attractive walk through typical Tyne Valley countryside starts at the Dipton Mill Inn and follows the Dipton Burn. It winds through deciduous woodland rich in birdsong and across pastures to a point where there are spectacular views across the Tyne Valley. Thence downhill over the 'bankses' and along a quaint 'lonnen' into Hexham. The return is by quiet lanes and over pastureland, passing the most beautiful racecourse in England and entering lovely Dipton Wood. Here in 1464 a kind-hearted robber sheltered Queen Margaret and her infant son in a cave after a battle during the Wars of the Roses.

The **Dipton Mill Inn** is a charming little pub which is also the tap for the local Hexhamshire Brewery. The main room is stone floored and has a beamed ceiling and a real fire.

There is a large garden with a stream running through it. Home brewed beers include Hexhamshire Devil's Elbow, Shire Bitter, Devil's Water, Whapweasel and Old Humbug. A wide variety of sandwiches and salads are available. Ploughman's lunch involves selecting from 14 cheeses, including most of the Northumbrian varieties. Food is home-cooked from local ingredients and served with fresh vegetables. A typical menu includes such items as haddock baked with tomato and basil, steak and kidney pie, chicken breast in sherry sauce and bacon chops in cider sauce. There are also home-made sweets such as fruit crumble, lemon tart and chocolate and rum truffle tart. The prices are reasonable.

Open from 12 pm to 2.30 pm and 6 pm to 11 pm Monday to Saturday and 12 pm to 3 pm and 7 pm to 10.30 pm on Sundays. Food is available daily from 12 pm to 2.30 pm and 6.30 pm to 8.30 pm.
☎ *01434 606577*

Distance – 5½ miles.

OS Explorer OL43 Hadrian's Wall, Haltwhistle and Hexham. GR 929610.
There are a couple of moderate inclines and some short stretches along quiet lanes.

Starting point The Dipton Mill Inn.

How to get there *Diptonmill is 2 miles south of Hexham. Take the B6306 to Blanchland and turn right towards Whitley Chapel but keep straight on to Diptonmill across a stone bridge at the bottom of a bank. There is a public parking area over the road from the pub.*

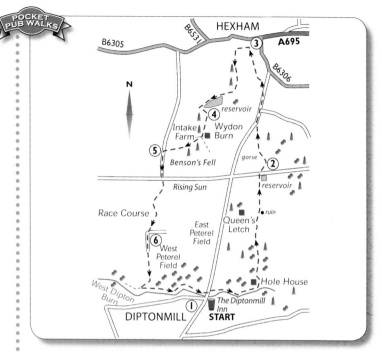

POCKET PUB WALKS

B6305 · B6531 · HEXHAM · A695 · ③ · B6306

N

reservoir
④ Wydon Burn
Intake Farm
⑤ Benson's Fell · gorse · ②
Rising Sun · reservoir
Race Course · ruin
East Peterel Field · Queen's Letch
⑥ West Peterel Field
West Dipton Burn · Hole House
① The Diptonmill Inn
DIPTONMILL · **START**

1 Cross the bridge, then the stile by the house on the right. Follow the track past paddocks, over a couple of stiles. Walk to the right of **Hole House** and over a little bridge. Follow the path into attractive woodland. Exit through a wicket gate into a field. Follow the right-hand boundary edge of three fields. At a stile signed **Newbiggin** (near **Queen's Letch Farm** where Queen Margaret's horse is said to have fallen – *letch* is an old word for slip) cross over and follow the left-hand boundary edge of two more fields. A final stile takes you onto a minor road. Cross this and a ladder stile. Beyond you can see **Hexham** and the **Tyne Valley**.

2 Follow the path down the left-hand edge of two fields and through gorse into a third field. At the far left corner of this field,

Hexham racecourse.

cross a stile onto a road. Turn right and walk to a junction. Cross over and turn down a narrow enclosed 'lonnen' starting beside the garden of the end house of **Elvaston Drive** and exit near the entrance gate of **Haining Croft** (a former hospital) at the top of **St Wilfred's Road**.

3 Turn left and walk past road ends into a dene (a regional term for a small wooded valley). Turn left, passing one bridge and then crossing a second bridge. Ascend from the dene to arrive at a children's playground. Circle this to the left and head for a complex of pigeon huts, or crees as they are known in the northeast. Follow a stony path between them and gardens to a road (signed **Wydon Park**). Turn left up a lane with allotments to your left. Within yards go through a kissing gate on your right. Follow a grassy path and, when it veers to the left, continue close to the reservoir and exit at a minor road.

4 Turn left, passing **Wydon Burn House**. At **Willowbrook House** follow the path to the left of the entrance to a road. Continue up this to **Intake Farm**. Go through the kissing gate (signed **Causey**

Hill) opposite. Follow the right-hand field edge for a hundred yards to cross a stile into a small wood. Follow the slippery path, with the burn on the right. Exit across a stile and continue upstream to reach a minor road.

5 Turn left and walk past **Benson's Fell** across a junction to the **Rising Sun cottage**. Cross a ladder stile (signed **West Dipton Burn**), then follow the left-hand field edge. Exit across a stile. In the next field bear right diagonally to cross the stile. **Hexham racecourse** is visible to the west. Cross the middle of the next field to a stile, then bear right over a fourth field to cross an awkward stile into a lane.

6 Turn right and walk to the right of **West Peterel Field**. Follow a right-hand field edge and enter another field. Follow the track across the field boundary, then cross a stile on the left into another field. Continue along the left-hand field edge, crossing another stile. The path descends into the **Dipton Burn** valley floor. At a path junction turn left and cross a stile into a field. Cross the field and go over a stile. Stay on the winding main path with **West Dipton Burn** over on your right. The path can be muddy in places, and there is an awkward stile. Exit through a kissing gate onto the road near **Dipton Mill Inn**.

Place of interest nearby

Hexham Abbey has been a place of worship since AD 674 when the first community was established by St Wilfrid. Many pillaged Roman stones were used in the building of the original abbey. The famous 7th-century crypt is open for tours at various times during the day. Also noteworthy are the Night Stairs, the Frith sanctuary stool and the painted Dance of Death in the High Altar area.
☎ 01434 602031

The Black Bull

Few walks have a Roman fortress at one end and a medieval castle at the other! A very attractive little Northumbrian town today, Corbridge actually has a military past. There was a large Roman base at this major Tyne crossing point before Hadrian's Wall was built. Stones from the old fort including a whole archway can be seen in St Andrew's church. Corbridge was once the capital of the kingdom of Northumbria. It was much damaged by Danish and Scottish raids, so not surprisingly there are two defensive pele towers. The Vicar's Pele, in the churchyard, is one of the best in the North. The walk starts along

Distance – 4½ miles.

OS Explorer OL43 Hadrian's Wall, Haltwhistle and Hexham. GR 989644.
This is level walking. It can be quite muddy and slippery in the Cor Burn valley. The A69 is crossed by means of a bridge.

Starting point The Black Bull at Corbridge.

How to get there Corbridge is near the junction of the A68 and the A69 or can be approached via the A695 from the south. The Black Bull stands in the centre of the main street. Park in the market place or down by the riverside. Alternatively, you could park at Aydon Castle and start the walk at point 3.

a quiet lane and bridleway at the edge of Corbridge and after crossing the A69 you follow a marked right of way over fields and along the lovely quiet valley of the Cor Burn. The return is over pasture and then down a fairly quiet road with the option of leaving that soon and returning down the bridleway. There are good views over the Tyne Valley.

THE PUB The **Black Bull** is in the centre of Corbridge. It was built in 1766 and has original stone floors and fireplaces. Beers on offer include Greene King, Black Sheep, Ruddles County and Old Speckled Hen. There is an extensive menu with bar meals such as smothered chicken and sweetcure bacon, beef and ale crown pie, slow-cooked lamb and four cheese and wild mushroom farfalle as well as Chef's Daily Specials. There is also a full array of light bites (quite substantial...) and a range of hot and cold sandwiches. For the sweet-toothed there are some smashing desserts. Ingredients are locally sourced and fresh. Prices are reasonable.

Open from 11 am to 11 pm from Monday to Saturday and 11.30 am to 11 pm on Sundays. Food is available from 12 pm to 3 pm and 6 pm to 9 pm (you would need to book for Sunday lunch though).
☎ *01434 632261*

1 From the **Black Bull** turn left and walk to the end of the main street. Turn left and walk up past the **Tourist Information Centre** and along the **Aydon Road** (B6321) to **Milkwell Lane** on your left, just past a primary school. Walk along the lane. After a few yards take a right fork into **Didridge Lane** (signed **Aydon Road/Aydon Castle**). Continue until you come to the **Corbridge-Hexham** bypass where the bridleway is diverted 500 yards eastwards to join **Aydon Road** and a bridge across the main road.

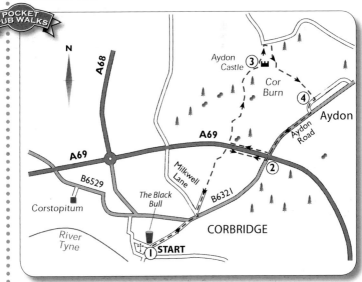

Aydon Castle is a 13th-century manor house.

2. Cross the bridge, then rejoin and follow the bridleway 500 yards to the west. You have excellent views across **Corbridge** and the **Tyne Valley**. Exit through a gate and continue ahead in a field with a wall and then a fence to the right. Go through a gate in the fenced section and bear half-left across the field to another gate into **Aydon Dene**. Descend to the **Cor Burn** on a clear path and cross the footbridge. Ascend the slope to **Aydon Castle** and exit the dene via a gate.

3. Follow the road past the castle and farm until you reach a stile over the stone wall on the right (signed **Aydon**). Cross this and descend into the dene to a footbridge over the **Cor Burn**.

Continue on the path until you reach and cross a complex double stile which gives access to a field at the top of the bank. The path continues to the right along the line of the fence bordering the dene. At the point where you cross a decayed hawthorn hedge boundary, turn left and walk across the field. Aim for the highest point in the field. You pass a marker post. **Aydon** comes into sight. Continue via an old stone gatepost to join a tractor road which will take you into **Aydon** village.

4 Turn right along the road through **Aydon**. This road joins the B6321. There is no pavement so walk on the verge where possible. Turn right on this quiet road and walk back towards **Corbridge**. You could stay on this road or (probably preferred) when you reach the bridge over the A69 you could retrace your steps down **Didridge Lane**.

Places of interest nearby

Aydon Castle (English Heritage), 1 mile north-east of Corbridge off the B6321 or the A68, is one of the finest 13th-century fortified manor houses in England, set in a beautiful landscape. Surviving virtually intact from the awful days of Border warfare, its roof is a great advantage for tourists on a wet Northumbrian day!
☎ 0870 608 2608

Corstopitum (English Heritage) provided essential support for Roman troops as they moved north or south and has everything a legion base should have – a water supply system, massive granaries, barracks, temples and a headquarters building where pay chests and military standards would be held and busy administrators churned out paperwork! There is also an extensive modern museum.
☎ 01434 632349

5 Haltwhistle

The Black Bull

Haltwhistle has a violent past. It might be all memorial gardens and flower beds today but it was once at the centre of the ongoing raiding, arson and murdering by border reivers. It stands in picturesque scenery and close to the Roman Wall yet it also had a very active industrial past – evidence of which will be seen on this walk. The name is derived from the Old French words *Haut Wisel* which mean *by two rivers*, and is inspired by the fact that the settlement stands in a fork of the South Tyne and the Haltwhistle Burn. You will enjoy some very good views of the Wall and the Whin Sill basalt ridge along which it is built, and the route crosses pastureland from and to the Roman Wall itself. The stretches along the Haltwhistle Burn are on good paths and tracks and include a long stepped descent. There are some small sections on very quiet lanes.

THE PUB

At the **Black Bull**, even the ostrich steak finished with nettle syrup uses local ingredients. This low, stone-built, whitewashed pub boasts an excellent range of six real ales. The lunch menu is extensive, imaginative and moderately priced. As well as the usual snacks you could encounter black pudding, Stilton and apple tower with Cumberland sauce, home-made salmon and dill fish cakes served on mixed salad with sweet chilli sauce, or traditional ploughman's, roast ham, two free range eggs and piles of home-cut chips. The evening menu is excellent and reasonably priced. Local fresh ingredients are used.

Open every day from 11 am to 11 pm. Food is served from 12 pm to 2 pm and 6 pm to 9 pm. For evening meals you are advised to book.
☎ *01434 320463*

Distance – 5 miles.

OS Explorer OL43 Hadrian's Wall, Haltwhistle and Hexham. GR 714643.
One long stepped descent and a busy road to cross.

Starting point The Black Bull in Haltwhistle.

How to get there *Haltwhistle is on the A69 west of Hexham. The Black Bull is in a side lane off the main street and you can park close by in the centre of the village.*

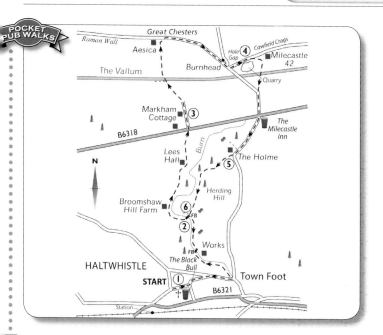

POCKET PUB WALKS

Great Chesters

Roman Wall

Aesica

The Vallum

Hole Gap (4) Cawfield Crags

Burnhead

Milecastle 42

Quarry

Markham Cottage (3)

The Milecastle Inn

B6318

Lees Hall

The Holme (5)

N

Herding Hill

Broomshaw Hill Farm

(6)

FB

(2)

Works

HALTWHISTLE

The Black Bull

Town Foot

START (1)

B6321

Station

1 From the **Black Bull** walk eastwards along the main street to **Town Foot Bridge**. From the near side of the bridge follow a lane upstream. At a parking area don't follow the path to the left but keep on ahead, on a grassy path along the edge of the burn. At another lane turn right and continue along a good path. When you meet another path turn right and walk to a minor road. Follow this past an old brickworks, then cross a works access bridge and turn left through a kissing gate. Take a left fork and reach a narrow footbridge.

2 Cross the bridge and turn right on a road. Ascend the road past **Broomshaw Hill Farm** and, going through two metal gates, pass round to the right of **Lees Hall Farm**. Another metal gate takes you onto a rough track. There are good views towards the Roman Wall here. Stay on this track to a gate onto the military

Cawfield Crags picnic site.

road (B6318), which you cross carefully to a track on the right side of a cottage.

3 Go down past **Markham Cottage**. Stay on this track until it bends sharp left, then turn right through a gate and walk towards **Great Chesters Farm**, crossing the site of the Roman fortress **Aesica** and passing a Roman altar on the right. In the field in front of the farm, cross a ladder stile over the right wall. Follow the line of the Roman Wall, crossing two more ladder stiles, and exit across a stile past **Burnhead Cottage** onto a minor road. Turn right and in a couple of yards turn left into the **Cawfield Crags** picnic site.

4 At **Cawfield** follow a fenced path along the north edge of the quarry lake. Go through two kissing gates just below **Milecastle 42**. From the second kissing gate a bridleway towards the south takes you onto a minor road leading to the picnic site. Walk up to the crossroads with the B6318, where you cross over onto the minor road to the right of the **Milecastle Inn**. Stay on this minor road and at the second signposted path (signed **Haltwhistle Burn**) cross the ladder stile.

5 | This path takes you over a low ridge, across pasture and past evidence of quarrying. Above on the left is a stone wall. When you reach a corner in that, bear right towards a fenced former quarry. Keep the fence on your right and join a grassy track to the edge of **Haltwhistle Burn** and a stone step stile. Cross the stile, pass a waymarked post and continue down the pasture towards **Herding Hill Farm**, where a waymarker directs you to a ladder stile.

6 | Cross the stile and follow the fence on your right to a wicket gate hidden in the wood edge. Go through and turn right along a path, then down a flight of steps to the valley floor. Turn left and follow the path to the works access bridge and back to **Town Foot**, retracing your steps to the **Black Bull**.

Places of interest nearby

The **Roman Army Museum** at Carvoran just off the B6318 stands on the Roman Wall. Visitors can do a virtual journey along the Wall, join the Roman army, dress up as a legionary or auxiliary and find out everything you always wanted to know about weapons, training, pay and recreation.

The museum is 15 minutes' drive from Roman **Vindolanda** where there are world famous civilian and military remains and on-going excavations, the Chesterholm Museum and several reconstructions of Roman buildings and a section of the Wall. There are cafés and shops at both. A joint admission price is available.

☎ 01434 344277; website: www.vindolanda.com

A bit nondescript bitey flies

Battlesteads Hotel

Tynedale was once, briefly, ruled by the kings of Scotland. Their court was held at Wark-on-Tyne (as opposed to Wark-on-Tweed), where there was a motte and bailey castle. As part of the estate of the Earl of Derwentwater, executed for his part in the 1715 Jacobite Rising, the manor was forfeited to the Crown and passed on to Greenwich Hospital, which put in naval chaplains as rectors. Nowadays it is a pleasant, unassuming grey stone village. Its agricultural connections are symbolised by the

Grey Bull Inn and Black Bull Inn next to each other. The small village green is not so obvious from the road which cuts through the middle of the village. It stands on the edge of the enormous Wark Forest, the largest wooded area in the Northumberland National Park and home to roe deer and red squirrels. Paths over pastureland take you up steadily onto the valley side above Wark. The return section is down a delightful quiet lane and then along the banks of the North Tyne back to the Battlesteads Hotel.

Distance – 3½ miles.

OS Explorer OL43 Hadrian's Wall, Haltwhistle and Hexham. GR 861770.
A couple of slight slopes but mostly level. An easy walk.

Starting point The roadside car park opposite the Battlesteads Hotel at Wark.

How to get there Wark is on the B6320, 3 miles south of Bellingham and 8 miles north of Hexham.

THE PUB Originally built as a farmstead in 1747, the family-run **Battlesteads Hotel** and restaurant near the banks of the North Tyne features an open fire, a sunny walled beer-garden, excellent bar meals and à la carte menus using fresh, local produce, a good choice of wines and a wide range of cask and bottle conditioned beers from local micro-breweries. Main beers are Black Sheep, Wylam, Nels Best, Durham Brewery and John Smith's. The owners have their own flock of sheep at Belsay, hence the Northumbrian lamb steak. Other temptations are warm salad of wild rabbit, black pudding and apple, poached salmon niçoise, twice-baked goats' cheese soufflé with chives and home-roasted ham. Those sheep appear again in the evening

Northumberland

menu with lamb cutlets, pan fried with leek roulade, minted new potatoes and rosemary gravy alongside fresh dressed crab and king prawn salad from North Shields Fish Quay and caramelised wild mushroom tart served with roast baby tomatoes and black-peppered sauté potatoes. There are also specials which change weekly and children's portions are available.

Open from 11 am to 11 pm . Lunch is served from 12 pm to 3 pm and dinner is served between 7 pm and 9.30 pm.
☎ *01434 230209; website: www.battlesteads-hotel.co.uk*

1 From **Battlesteads** turn left, walk into the village centre and turn left to walk west along the road signposted **Stonehaugh** and **Wygate**. Pass allotments on the left, then turn left through a kissing gate (signed **Ramshaw's Mill**) next to a corrugated iron shed. Follow the path, over a burn and up a grassy slope. When the path divides, stay close to the left field edge. Cross an old field boundary, then go through a gate near Scots pines.

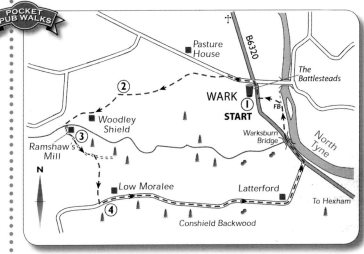

Ramshaw's Mill.

Continue on towards a barn but cross a step stile on the left just before it.

2 Walk half-right over the field to the buildings of **Woodley Shield** but bear right before you reach them to a ladder stile, which you cross to join a track. Follow this until you come to the second telegraph pole, which has a waymarker on the left side. Leave the track and, bearing right over a field, walk down to cross a stile onto a road. Turn left and cross the bridge beside **Ramshaw's Mill**.

3 Ignore a footpath sign to the right and stay on the track to curve round behind the buildings and then through a wooden gate

Northumberland

into oak woodland. Follow the fairly steep path until you reach a marker post. Take the left marker to follow a line of oak trees. At the end of these take a sharp right turn on a short track up to a gate. Go through this and then down the left side of the next field with a wall alongside you, through a gate and then through another gate onto a minor lane beside **Low Moralee Farm**.

4 Turn left along the lane. Follow this quiet and most attractive lane for about a mile, passing through **Latterford Farm**. At the junction with the B6320 turn left and walk very carefully along the road for about 600 yards. Cross the bridge over **Warks Burn** and at a footpath sign to **Wark**, turn right through a haulage yard and follow the footpath along the bank of the **North Tyne**. Cross a footbridge, turn left and walk past an impressive old schoolhouse on the right to exit onto the road near the **Battlesteads Hotel**.

Place of interest nearby

Just to the north of Wark is the **Bellingham Heritage Centre**, which stands in the grounds of the former railway station just a few hundred yards from the village centre. The Heritage Centre preserves and displays the history of the North Tyne and Redesdale area of Northumberland. Exhibitions include the Border Counties Railway, the evocative photographs of the 1920s and 1930s of W. P. Collier, the mines and quarries and the border reivers. Family history researchers can access a database of over 30,000 names. Using an old red telephone box you can dial and listen to the oral reminiscences of local people. You can even try on the helmets of border reivers for size!

☎ 01434 220050; website: www.bellingham-heritage.org.uk

The Sun Inn

Morpeth is the busy county town of Northumberland and this walk is from castle to castle. It starts beneath Morpeth Castle (mostly 15th-century) in Castle Walk on the edge of the attractive Carlisle Park and then goes along the riverside to ruined Mitford Castle. It takes you through meadows, over pasture, through mixed and deciduous woodland and along quiet lanes. Despite the close proximity of the A1 bypass (which you go under) and bustling Morpeth, there is surprisingly quiet and restful countryside to explore in this walk.

Distance – 6 miles.

OS Explorer 325 Morpeth and Blyth. GR 197852.
Level apart from a couple of short stretches.

Starting point The Sun Inn at Morpeth.

How to get there Leave the A1 at Clifton to follow the A197 into Morpeth. The Sun Inn stands on the left just past the church of St Mary the Virgin. You can park in the pub car park, with the permission of the landlord.

THE PUB **The Sun** is a 19th-century inn standing on the main road into Morpeth. It is traditional in style and character and very popular locally. Beers on offer are John Smith's, McEwan and Fosters whilst guest beers include Adnam's Broadside and Marston's Fever Pitch. There is a wide-ranging menu of main courses and snacks, at a range of prices. Local ingredients are used. As well as the traditional dishes, there are tempting specials such as Barbary duck breast with rosemary, fresh monkfish wrapped in Parma ham and fillet steak and asparagus salad. The sweet-toothed need not go away unsatisfied with items such as Chocolate Humpy Bumpy on the list, as well as all the usual suspects.

Open from 11.30 am to 11 pm every day. The weekday menu is available from 12 pm to 2 pm and 6 pm to 9 pm. Sunday lunches are served from 12 pm to 6 pm.
☎ *01670 514153*

1 From the **Sun**, turn left and at the post box turn left up the path to join the old A1 (now A197). Turn right and follow this and a raised walkway to exit at **Castle Square**. Walk between **Benfield Motors** and the **Joiners Arms** and then follow the very

pleasant riverside path from **Carlisle Park** to its end. You pass a footbridge, go under **Oldgate Bridge** and then pass another footbridge. At **Low Ford Bridge** join the road.

2 Turn left on the road and then left up a lane to **Abbotswood Cottage** (signed **Mitford** and **Kirkhill**). At the cottage, go through a kissing gate, then another and follow the path to **High House Lane**. Cross the road and take the path over a small bridge, through two kissing gates, following signs to **Mitford** with the river always to your right. All is peace and birdsong until you approach the bypass viaduct.

3 Follow the path left, uphill, then walk under the viaduct and go up steps and over a stile into a field. Follow the trees on your right. Where they end, aim for a stile in the right-hand corner of the field (more or less in the same line). Cross the stile and walk down over the footbridge, with a very pleasant stretch of the river on your right. Join the road at **Mitford Bridge**.

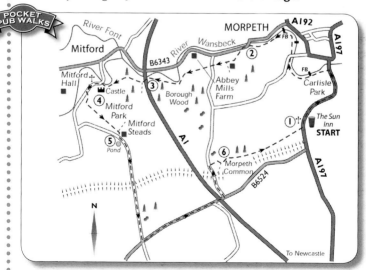

Mitford Castle.

4 Walk left along the road, past the church, then cross a stile into **Castle Field** (signed **Mitford Steads**). Pass an old block house, then cross a decayed hump-backed farm bridge and walk up alongside trees to a stile. From here, aim for the left end of conifers on the far side of the large field. Cross the ladder stile there and then keep on with the fence on your right. Just before **Mitford Steads**, turn right to cross a stile (signed **Mitford** and **Borough Woods**), cross a small meadow and then exit over a stile onto the quiet road.

5 Turn left and walk down the lane, passing a pond on the right. The pleasant country lane intersects with the busy B6524. Turn left along this and head towards **Morpeth**. Use the verge, where possible. Past a factory go under a flyover, then turn left up **High House Lane**. Turn right after a bridge at a **Morpeth** sign and bear right, ignoring a clear footpath down to the abandoned railway line and following a more overgrown path to the left of that through the wood to emerge into playing fields.

6 | Stay on the right of the playing fields. Go through a kissing gate beside a field gate and then continue across the middle of the ridge and furrow of **Morpeth Common**. Leave this through a kissing gate and go between a cemetery and pitch and putt course. Stay on this track alongside the churchyard until you reach a small stone building (a viewpoint from which body-snatchers might be seen!). Just past that, enter **St Mary's churchyard** via a gap. The churchyard contains the grave of suffragette Emily Davison. At the church, turn right to the road and the **Sun Inn**.

Places of interest nearby

Ten miles from Morpeth is **Belsay Hall** (English Heritage). Beautiful 30-acre gardens link the medieval tower-house castle and Jacobean mansion ruins to the dramatic Greek revival Belsay Hall built in 1807. The tea room is open in summer as well.
☎ 01661 881636

Children might prefer the **Whitehouse Farm Centre** just off the A197 to the south-west of Morpeth. You can feed and stroke various animals to your heart's content. There is a good soft-play area, pedal tractors and tractor rides.
☎ 01670 789998; website: www.whitehousefarmcentre.co.uk

The Anglers Arms

Weldon is a hamlet on the north bank of the lovely Coquet, just off the A697 and on the road to Rothbury. It consists of a handful of cottages, a converted mill house and the famous Northumbrian coaching inn – and rather anomalously a Pullman railway carriage attached to the latter. It is a scenic place with an attractive 18th-century bridge in front of the inn. This walk takes you through very quiet rolling countryside and farmland on the banks of the middle reaches of the Coquet. This is *heugh* and *haugh* countryside! Many of the place-names are suffixed thus. A *heugh* is a height by a river, perhaps a cliff or crag or just a steep bank. A *haugh* is a meadow within the arms of a bank or heights. As a result, and confusingly, you often find the two together, and especially in a river valley such as the Coquet.

Weldon Walk 8

The **Anglers Arms**, an attractive, whitewashed, 18th-century former coaching inn on the banks of the Coquet, is embellished with memorabilia of 'hunting, shooting and fishing'. The main house ales are Greene King Abbot Ale, Timothy Taylor and Co Landlord and Abbot and Wells Bombardier. The menu is extensive. Local ingredients are used as much as possible, e.g. home-made steak and ale pie, Northumbrian sausage casserole, roasted rack of Border lamb and even the blackened cajun salmon. There are light (substantial) meals in the form of home-made bread and rolls with various fillings and chips, fresh garden leaf salads and a vegetarian selection, including the tempting wild mushroom and capsicum stroganoff. The cheese menu includes Northumberland with Nettles. Check the specials board as well in case you miss items like venison and whiskey sauce. You can dine in the à la carte Pullman railway carriage if you wish. Prices are reasonable.

Open 11 am to 11 pm on weekdays and Saturdays and 12 pm to 10.30 pm on Sundays. Food is served throughout these times.
☎ *01665 570271/570655; website: www.anglersarms.com*

Distance – 4½ miles.

OS Explorer 325 Morpeth and Blyth. GR 137985.
Level and easy. There is some walking on very quiet roads, and one very busy road to cross.

Starting point The Anglers Arms at Weldon.

How to get there *Weldon is near the junction of the A697 and the B6344 and is about 7 miles from Rothbury and 10 miles north of Morpeth. Park by the roadside in the hamlet.*

1 From the front of the **Anglers Arms**, turn left and walk up the road to the junction. Turn right there and go under the road bridge. Follow the slip road round to the right and then turn left to follow a farm track through **Weldon Wood** to **Low** and **High Weldon**. It turns sharp right at **Low Weldon**. At **High Weldon** it goes between buildings and over a lawn, the route marked helpfully by a line of small conifers, then through a wicket gate onto another farm track.

2 Continue past a barn on the right and through two gates towards the **River Coquet**. Cross a field next to the river and head to the left of an isolated cottage at the bottom of a hill. With bracken and gorse to your right, ascend the slope. At the top follow a footpath through a gate within the left-hand edge of some

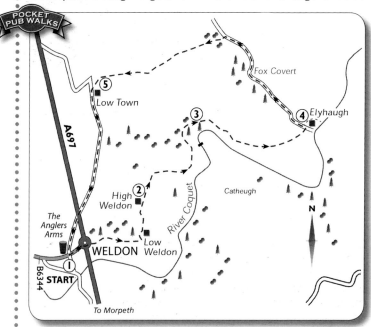

POCKET
PUB WALKS

Fox Covert

⑤
Low Town

③
④ Elyhaugh

A697

High ②
Weldon
Catheugh

The
Anglers
Arms

N

WELDON
Low
Weldon

River Coquet

B6344
① START

To Morpeth

Elyhaugh Farm, near Weldon.

woods and then a second waymarked gate on the left into a field – ignore a smaller path to the right.

3 Walk on along the right-hand edge of the field and then through another waymarked gate into a second field. Walk across the middle of this (on the slightly raised bank) towards a group of oak trees on the far side. Cross a stile beside a field gate and then follow the right-hand edge of another field, crossing yet another stile to enter a small field next to the impressive **Elyhaugh Farm**. Built in 1737, its architectural features show how classical forms penetrated into the countryside – if you had enough money! Go through a wicket gate and turn left through a gate to join a farm road (another wicket gate gives public access to the attractive banks of the **Coquet** – its peacefulness disturbed only by the occasional silvery trout or ungainly heron).

4 Follow the farm road for ½ mile. Walk on past the plantation known as **Fox Covert**, where the track turns sharp right and then left again. Turn left at a signpost to **Low Town** through a field gate within a thin belt of woodland (opposite a double field gate). Follow the field edge on the right and exit into a small copse through a field gate. Keep the same line through the copse and then exit across a stile to cross two fields with the hedges on your left. Go through one field gate and then over a stile by a double gate.

5 This brings you to **Low Town Farm** and onto a track (signed back to **Picklewood**). Follow this for a few yards onto a metalled road (the old A697). Turn left and follow what is now a very quiet and pleasant road. It takes you down to the busy and fast A697 road which you must cross carefully. Follow the slip road back to **Weldon** and the **Anglers Arms**.

Place of interest nearby

Brinkburn Priory (English Heritage) is only a couple of miles away on the Rothbury road (B6344). This is a fully roofed and restored idyllic riverside Augustinian priory church, which is a marvellous example of early Gothic architecture. It dates from the 12th century. You can also explore the adjacent empty manor house and find more evidence of the medieval monastery to which the church belonged. A prominent bell sculpture commemorates the story that the monks were so overjoyed when Scottish raiders overlooked the priory in a dense mist that they rang the bell to celebrate – and the raiders heard and returned!
☎ 01665 570628

9 **Thropton**

The Three Wheat Heads

There are **splendid panoramic** vistas of Coquetdale and the curiously-shaped Simonside Hills, which were the focus for Iron Age religious rituals, on this walk. Thropton is a small village on the banks of the Coquet and the route takes you away from the river, over moors and through woodland along well marked paths and tracks. At different points you have bird's-eye views of Thropton and Rothbury. This is achieved with little real effort since height is gained very easily. With views like this and the lonely sound of the curlews and the vivid purple heather, the only other thing you need is the evocative sound of the Northumbrian pipes – and indeed some of the most famous exponents of this instrument are from Coquetdale.

The **Three Wheat Heads** is a 300-year-old inn in the centre of Thropton. Its main beers are Theakston's, John Smith's and Black Sheep. As well as sandwiches, salads and a good children's menu, the main courses on offer include a range of fish and steak dishes, pork stroganoff, braised lamb shank, rack of Northumbrian lamb, chicken Belle Claire, game casserole and steak and mushroom pie. The Three Wheat Heads Challenge mixed grill may require more time than you have available. There is also a good vegetarian menu.

Open 11 am to 3 pm Monday to Thursday (food available 12 pm to 2.30 pm) and 6 pm to 11 pm (food available 6 pm to 9 pm). Friday evening opening is 5 pm but the meal times are the same. Saturday 11 am to 11 pm (food available 12 pm to 9 pm) and Sunday 12 pm to 10.30 pm (food available 12 pm to 9 pm).
☎ *01669 620262*

1 From the front of the **Three Wheat Heads** turn right and walk up the B6341 past the **Cross Keys** and turn left into **Physic Lane**. Follow this through a wooden gate and on between trees and hedgerows. Go through a metal gate and alongside a dry-stone wall on the edge of a coniferous plantation. Pass through a wooden gate and follow the path by a wall on the right and then left up an incline to another wooden gate. Go through this.

Distance – 5½ miles.

OS Explorer 332 Alnwick and Amble. GR 027023.
An initial gradual rise, the rest is level and downhill.

Starting point The Three Wheat Heads in Thropton.

How to get there Thropton is 2 miles west of Rothbury on the B6341. The Three Wheat Heads is in the middle of the village and you can park there with the permission of the landlord. There is also limited roadside parking.

POCKET PUB WALKS

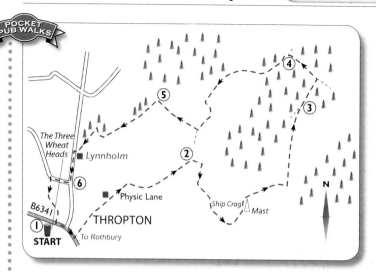

The Three Wheat Heads
■ Lynnholm

B6341

■ Physic Lane

THROPTON

Ship Crag △ Mast

To Rothbury

① START

N

2 Cross the track in front of you and turn right on a rocky path which takes you to a stony track, where you turn right. Follow it round **Ship Crag**, passing a prominent mast to your right, and approach a large wooden gate with a kissing gate beside it and woodland beyond. A few yards in front of the gates there is a waymarked post pointing to the left. Follow an obvious sandy path towards extensive woodland past an isolated wicket gate and across two footbridges. Go through a wicket gate into the coniferous plantation.

3 Walk up the path and turn right on a wider forest track. Ignore intersecting tracks to the left and walk on to forestry wooden gates (probably open) through which you join an unsurfaced road and turn left at a sign pointing towards **Snitter**. At the next wooden gate (signed left to **Thropton/Rothbury**) turn left in front of the facing gate and go through another gate on the left.

4 Follow the track through open woodland, passing a stone-walled plantation on the right. The track swings to the left. Ignore a

couple of minor paths to the right. After a sharp left turn the track bends to the right. On this return curve, turn right on another track cutting across the main track. Follow this towards a dry-stone wall to the right. Where another track joins from the left, go through a gap in the wall to your right. Walk towards a pair of stone gate posts, then turn right with the field boundary on the left. Follow this to arrive at a fence at the bottom of a steep slope.

5 Turn left and follow this fence along a bridleway, keeping it to your right. Go through a wicket gate and then through a wider gate onto a green lane. Follow the lane along an avenue of thorn trees. Stay on it as it bends to the right and then to the left, through a couple of metal gates and then joins a surfaced lane. Turn right along this lane and walk via **Lynnholm** down to a minor road. Turn left on this road and walk to a road junction.

6 Turn right here and walk to a road bridge and go through a kissing gate (signed **Thropton Bridge**). Follow a path bearing away from the stream at first and then back towards it. Cross a small wooden footbridge and go through a kissing gate to join a path amongst trees above the stream, then another kissing gate into a grassy area attached to a private garden. Keep to the right to reach another kissing gate and wooden steps to the road and **Thropton Bridge**. Turn right back into **Thropton**.

Place of interest nearby

Cragside (National Trust) is 1 mile north of Rothbury off the B6341. This breathtaking Victorian house was the creation of Lord Armstrong, the famous Victorian inventor and munitions manufacturer. It was the first house in the world to be lit by electricity.
☎ 01669 620150; website: www.nationaltrust.org.uk

The Plough

Alnwick is well known for the picturesque Hotspur Gate which guards access to its central bustling marketplace. The many interesting shops and inns include one of the largest secondhand bookshops in England and the White Swan Hotel, whose Olympic Room is panelled with woodwork salvaged from the sister ship of the *Titanic*. On this walk through Hulne Park you pass through attractive woodland and over pasture and ornamental parkland with lovely views of the River Aln and of wooded hillsides. There is a very scenic ruined priory. You may see red squirrels, deer and shaggy highland cattle. The park is open from 11 am to sunset (01665 510777). No dogs are allowed in the park.

THE PUB

The **Plough** is an ornate Victorian inn on the site of a much older hostelry which dated back to the 17th century. It is atmospheric with original woodwork and fittings. Beers on offer are changed regularly to provide variation, e.g. Stone's, Deuchars, Greene King, Mordue's and Hadrian and Border. It is well known locally for good substantial down-to-earth food and is also a popular folk music venue. Local ingredients are used. Main courses include steaks, the Plough mini grill, Plough cottage pie, chicken and mushroom pie and Northumbrian bangers and mash. There is a fish menu and a vegetarian menu. In addition there is a very wide variety of light lunches available such as soups, brunch, Plough toad in the hole, and fish and chips.

Opening times are 11 am to 11 pm on weekdays and 11 am to 10.30 pm on Sundays. Food is served between 12 pm and 3 pm and 6 pm and 9 pm.
☎ *01665 602395*

Distance – 5 miles

OS Explorer 332 Alnwick and Amble.
GR 185138.
A level walk – unless you choose to visit Hulne Priory on the way, which is well worth it.

Starting point The Plough at Alnwick.

How to get there *Alnwick is just off the A1. You enter the town centre through the famous Hotspur Gate. The Plough is on the right as you approach the gateway. For the public car park and public toilets nearby, turn right at the traffic lights at the gateway.*

1. From the **Plough** turn right and walk through the **Hotspur Gate** and along the main street of **Alnwick**. Bear right up to the castle. With your back to the castle entrance, walk along the road, passing **St Michael's church**, which is completely Perpendicular in style, then ahead along a leafy lane, **Rotten Row**, to the entrance to **Hulne Park**. Follow the road (**Farm Drive**) beneath an arch. At a waymarker post on the right, turn right.

2. Walk down the stony path to join a track. Turn right along the track and walk on until you reach a forked junction marked with a large tree and a signpost-boulder. Take the left fork. Then follow the track alongside the river through very pleasant woodland.

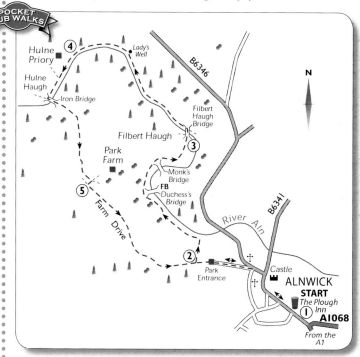

The remains of Hulne Priory.

On the right you pass a footbridge, the **Duchess's Bridge**, which is partly hidden by trees. At a junction keep right and continue. Exit the woodland through a wide gate into parkland but stay on the track. Walk past the **Monk's Bridge** and across **Filbert Haugh**.

3 Pass through a gate. At **Filbert Haugh Bridge**, cross the **River Aln**. Continue left along the track (**Lady's Well Drive**) through pastureland with the river on your left. Pass through another gate and re-enter the woodland. Stay with the riverside track passing on the right the **Lady's Well** and then a suspension footbridge on the left. Proceed ahead and eventually exit into an extensive meadow.

[4] Walk on with the remains of **Hulne Priory** (usually open to the public) to the right above you and the river to the left. This was one of the earliest English Carmelite priories, founded around 1240. The defensive wall was not for decoration! Monasteries were tempting targets for border raiders. Go through a gate to reach the **Iron Bridge** which you cross leaving the red waymarked route. Follow the track across pastureland through a series of wooden gates. When you reach a metalled farm road, turn right and walk along it for a few yards to the park road.

[5] Turn left along the park road. Ignore side tracks and roads to left and right. The road passes over a bridge. Finally you will arrive at the arch which you passed beneath at the beginning of the walk. Stay on the road until you reach the junction and then return past **Alnwick Castle** to the start.

Places of interest nearby

Alnwick Castle, set in a stunning landscape, is one of the great fortresses of Europe. It has been a film location for many productions including *Harry Potter* and *Blackadder*. The many attractions and exhibitions include the story of knighthood (… and if you are young enough you can dress up, learn to use a sword and face the Quest!). There is also an excellent castle shop and a splendid restaurant.
☎ 01665 510777; website: www.alnwickcastle.com

The **Alnwick Garden** is one of the most exciting contemporary gardens to be developed in the last century. It is a magical place created with children very much in mind, and there is an enormous tree house, as well as water features. Getting wet is a compulsory part of the programme!
☎ 01665 511350; website: www.alnwickgarden.com

11 Eglingham

The Tankerville Arms

Eglingham **(pronounced** *Eglingjum***)** was described in 1886 as 'a pretty and colourful village with many remarkable instances of longevity and with a genial and invigorating air that gives increased health to the strong and imparts new life to those whose physical energies have temporarily deteriorated.' Despite the arcadian scenery there were once collieries and quarries here. The names Tarry Lane and Tarry House commemorate a colliery at the top of the lovely tree-lined lane and tar was a by-product. There are excellent views of the Cheviots and Beanley Moor with its early warning 'golf ball' throughout this walk, and at the expense of little uphill effort. Footpaths through old deciduous woodland, along the edges of arable fields and over pleasant pastures and very quiet and enjoyable country lanes make up most of this walk.

THE PUB

The stone-built **Tankerville Arms**, with original beams, dates from 1830, albeit on the site of a much older inn. The main beers are John Smith, Hadrian and Border, Mordue's and Black Sheep. The staff are very friendly and accommodating. The same menu is available in both the restaurant and the bar. The cost of meals is rather more than you might pay for standard bar meals – but is well worth it! Typical dishes are salmon on herb-baked tomatoes with melted gruyère cheese, cod on a fennel potato bake, pork chunk with apple and onion ragout, and cannon of venison on chunky black pudding with roasted leeks. There is a good vegetarian menu. Specials are added on a daily basis. A mouth-watering range of desserts is worth exploring. There is also a beer garden with lovely views.

Opening times are Monday to Thursday 12 pm to 2 pm and 6.30 pm to 11 pm. On Friday and Saturday the evening is extended to 12.30 am. Sunday evening times are 6.30 pm to 10.30 pm. Food is served every day during these times.
☎ *01665 578444*

Distance – 4½ miles.

OS Explorer 332 Alnwick and Amble. GR 106196.
A couple of very gradual uphill sections. Some walking along very quiet lanes.

Starting point The Tankerville Arms at Eglingham.

How to get there *Eglingham is on the B6346, which links with the A697 to Wooler and with the B6341 at Alnwick. It lies 8 miles to the north-west of Alnwick. The Tankerville Arms stands in the middle of the village. You can park outside the inn with the permission of the landlord. Otherwise there is some roadside parking.*

1 Starting from the **Tankerville Arms**, turn right down the main street, cross a bridge and walk on a few yards to a bridleway sign on the right (**Eglinghammoor**). Cross over the road and go up the drive of the house opposite the sign which is a right of way. Ignore the wicket gate in front of you but turn right and go through a wide wooden gate. Follow a grassy track alongside a coniferous plantation. Go through the gate in the right-hand corner into another field. Stay on the same line to the top of a bank. Then head to the right and follow the field edge to the corner. There turn left and follow the fence line to the top corner of the field. Go through the first of two metal gates and, in the field beyond, walk along the top edge with the hedge to your left. Go through a waymarked rusty metal gate on your left to join a farm track. Follow this to another gate which takes you onto a road opposite the drive to **Eglinghamhill Farm**.

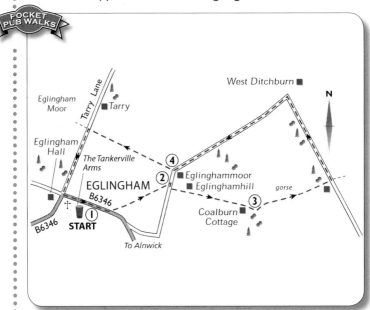

Tarry.

2 Turn right, then left, down a lane, passing the front of the farm. Continue on through a series of four gates until you come to **Coalburn Cottage**. Follow a narrow overgrown footpath by a hedge on your left and a woodpile on the right, entering old deciduous woods and crossing the stream on a wooden footbridge. Continue ahead until you exit through a wicket gate. Ignore another wicket gate on your right.

3 Through the gate, turn right and follow the fence on your right. Continue over rough pasture and through gorse, following a grassy path and passing a couple of wicket gates on the right. Go through a wide metal gate near a barn beside a large house (not shown on the OS map) then down a short lane to a road where you turn left. You come to a metalled lane. Turn left onto

this and stay with it, turning sharp left beside **West Ditchburn** and arriving at **Eglinghammoor Farm** opposite a coniferous plantation, where a bridleway sign points to **Harehope**.

4 Follow the bridleway track through a series of five gates until you reach **Tarry Lane**. There are some lovely views of the **Cheviots** and **Beanley Moor** on this section. Turn left down leafy **Tarry Lane** and walk down to **Eglingham village**. Arriving at the main street again you turn left and walk back to the **Tankerville Arms**. On the way, call in to have a look around **St Maurice's church**.

Places of interest nearby

Chillingham Castle, north of Eglingham on the B6346, is the most haunted castle in Britain. Since the 13th century it has been continuously owned by the Grey family. The castle has intriguing interiors, arms and armour, torture chamber, dungeons, Italian ornamental gardens and woodland walks. There are tea rooms and a gift shop.
☎ 01668 215359; Website: www.chillingham-castle.com
While there you might also want to see the famous wild cattle of **Chillingham Park**, the only cattle in the world to have remained free of any breeding management. Access to the park is permitted only by arrangement and when escorted by the warden since the cattle are unpredictable and dangerous.
☎ 01668 215250;
Website: www.chillingham-wildcattle.org.uk

The Dunstanburgh Castle Hotel

Embleton is the gateway to one of the finest beaches in Northumberland as well as an attractive village. Close to the little green is the Old Manse (now a private residence), with a plaque commemorating the fact that this was the birthplace of the famous crusading journalist, William Thomas Stead, who played a prominent role in the struggle against child prostitution and died on the *Titanic* in April 1912. Near the route is Dunstan Steads, where the famous theologian Duns Scotus was born, and from an insulting comment about whom the word 'dunce' is derived! The deceptive Holy Trinity church is actually largely 13th-century, albeit with a Victorian veneer. The first stretch of this relaxing stroll is along the edge of a golf course towards Dunstanburgh Castle, which dominates the walk for most of the

Distance – 5½ miles.

OS Explorer 332 Alnwick and Amble. GR 232225.
This route is level and easy. There are alternative outward paths along the sand dunes (challenging) or along the beach if the tide is out.

Starting point The Dunstanburgh Castle Hotel, Embleton.

How to get there *Travelling north on the A1, take the B1340 north of Alnwick and approach Embleton via Denwick and Rennington. Heading south, follow the B1342 from Belford to Bamburgh and then the B1339 to Embleton. You can park in the village centre.*

route and which so mesmerised the artist Turner. The rest is over pleasant pastureland and along field edges.

THE PUB The **Dunstanburgh Castle Hotel**, in the middle of Embleton, is a large family-run traditional hotel, with a relaxed atmosphere. The main beers on offer are Theakston's, Boddington's and Tetley's. It is open to non-residents. Light snacks available include a good variety of sandwiches and toasted pannini, various salads and cream teas. The hotel kitchen caters for a wide variety of tastes and makes full use of the best local produce such as fresh seafood from Seahouses, Scottish salmon, Cheviot lamb and Craster kippers. Servings err towards the substantial.

The bar is open from 11 am to 11 pm. Lunches are available between 12 pm and 2 pm and dinner from 7 pm to 8.30 pm. Light snacks are available between 12 pm and 6 pm.
☎ *01665 576111*

Embleton Walk 12

1 From the village square and with the **Dunstanburgh Castle Hotel** to your left, walk up **Front Street**, **Dunstanburgh Terrace** and down the enclosed and raised path alongside a lane to the **Dunstanburgh Castle Golf Club**. Pass the clubhouse on the left, open to non-members for parking (a small charge) and for drinks and meals, and go through a wicket gate.

2 Turn right onto the course and skirt round some rushes to cross a footbridge to your right on the golf course. Then bear right to follow the waymarked coast path along the edge of the course, with a hedge to the right. You pass a small copse of trees on the left and a sign about **Dunstanburgh Castle** at the end of a lane.

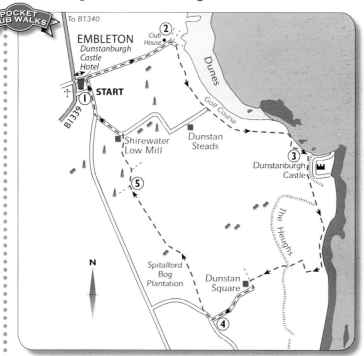

POCKET PUB WALKS

Dunstanburgh Castle.

Continue alongside fenced fields, ignoring a path coming in from the left, until a waymarked post directs you over the end section of the golf course. This (and the other routes) brings you to a kissing gate with a National Trust marker. Continue on towards **Dunstanburgh Castle**. Stay on the lower path.

3 Beneath the castle, the path takes you past a blockhouse above on the left and across a short causeway towards a kissing gate. Go through and continue on to the next fence. Go through the wicket gate. Turn right here and follow the fence on your right to go through another wide gate, where you turn right and walk past gorse to another gate that gives you access to open land. Turn left and follow the track between thick gorse, past a gate on the left, then through a facing field gate and onto the farm lane of **Dunstan Square** through a final gate signposted to **Craster** and **Dunstanburgh Castle**. Turn left and follow the lane past a farm and cottages to a junction with a road.

4. At the road turn right. As the road soon turns left, take a track off to the right (signposted to **Dunstan Steads** and **Embleton**). The very clear track goes across the field to a corner where there is a bridge and a stile obscured by trees. Cross the bridge and stile and follow a path to the left along the edge of a wood. At the end of the field, go through a gate and keep on along the right-hand side of a hedge. Pass a seasonal caravan and campsite on the left and cross a stile at the end of the field. At this point bear right to cross a bridge onto a clear path through some woods.

5. Turn right and walk down to a field gate and stile on the left. Cross the stile and go over the field to another stile and wicket gate. Cross the stile and then bear right down a dip, through a gate and then turn left to go through a gate and over a bridge. Walk up to the road and turn left to walk up to a junction where you turn right and return to **Embleton village**.

Place of interest nearby

Howick Hall Gardens are just a couple of miles south of Craster. Howick Hall stands in a lovely dene and has extensive grounds notable for mixed woodland, fine flower gardens and beautiful shrubs. They are especially worth visiting in the daffodil season. The Hall is the ancestral home of a branch of the Grey family which played a significant role in British politics. Earl Grey, whose statue dominates the centre of Newcastle, orchestrated the passing of the Great Reform Act of 1832 which began the move towards popular democracy. There is also a smashing restaurant. The grounds and restaurant are open from Easter to October from 12 noon to 6 pm. While in the area you could buy some of those wood-smoked kippers for which Craster is famous.
☎ 01665 577285

The Tankerville Arms Hotel

'**Windy Wooler' on the River Glen** was originally an agricultural market town but developed in the 19th century as the gateway to the beautiful Cheviots with their invigorating air. A local doctor wrote a book of walks in 1926, arguing that a holiday at Wooler was a health cure: 'The kind of case for which Wooler is pre-eminently suited is simply that of the person who is in need of rest and recreation, either in consequence of prolonged overwork, or of illness … Wooler is capable of being at once a haven of rest and a cornucopia of fresh vigour …'. Its modest demeanour must be seen in the context of an area notable for a high density of pre-Roman settlements, the first battle of the legendary King Arthur, a great royal stronghold of the Saxon kings of Northumbria, the work of St Paulinus in converting the area to Christianity and recurrent border fighting, which has left its mark on the landscape in different ways. On this walk you will encounter some of the famous enigmatic cup-and-ring stone markings which were left by prehistoric peoples in various parts of Northumberland. You follow a well-trodden, gently rising, winding path through bracken to Weetwood Moor. After an easy walk across the flat moorland you return via quiet lanes and broad tracks.

Distance – 6 miles

OS Explorer 340 Holy Island and Bamburgh. GR 989283. A gradual, easy ascent followed by flat moorland walking, then descending on quiet lanes and tracks.

Starting point The Tankerville Arms in Wooler.

How to get there *Wooler stands on the A697 and is about 15 miles to the north-west of Alnwick. The Tankerville Arms is on the northern edge of the town on South Road (the A697). Park at the pub or in the main town car park in Padgepool Place beside the Tourist Information Centre and the Primary Care Trust building.*

THE PUB

The **Tankerville Arms Hotel** is a privately-owned traditional coaching inn fronting the A697 out of Wooler to the north, with a beer garden and good parking. The main beers are John Smith's and Hadrian and Border. You can get bar food, including main courses and salads, sandwiches and a children's menu. Main courses include items such as the Tankerville mixed platter, Craster kipper pâté, fresh local cod, and grilled lamb chops. There is also a dinner menu served in the restaurant which may include dishes like breast of duck and Aberdeen Angus steaks.

The pub is open from 11 am to 11 pm. Food is served daily from 12 noon to 2 pm and from 6.30 pm to 9 pm.
☎ *01668 281581; website: www.tankervillehotel.co.uk*

1 Turn left from the **Tankerville Arms** and walk down **South Road** (the A697) passing a garage and **Weetwood Bridge**. Walk along the grass beside the river to the stone road bridge. Cross this and walk ahead past the Riverside Bar on the left and Bridgend chalet and caravan site on the right, then along

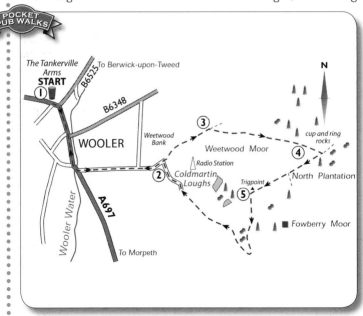

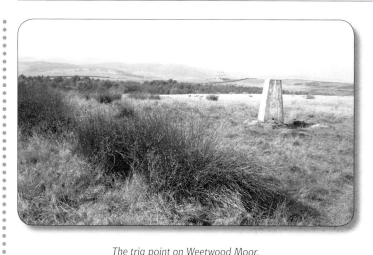

The trig point on Weetwood Moor.

Brewery Lane past a school on the left. Walk up a bank to a signpost on the left to **Weetwood Moor**. This is also on the route of **St Cuthbert's Way**.

[2] From the signpost, follow a clear path which winds up easily through bracken, through a wicket gate and into a wildlife conservation area. There are excellent views over **Wooler** and the **Cheviots**. All this with little effort. Keep on along the path until you arrive at the top and a waymarked post.

[3] There is a very obvious grassy path ahead and another lesser one bearing to the right. Follow the lesser one. The OS map and the waymarkers tell slightly different stories. Ahead of you over the moor you will see three plantations. Aim for the right-hand end of the middle one. This path will take you there although it gradually diminishes into a much narrower one in thick heather. Keep left at a fork and straight over at a cross-paths. Pass small cairns and an isolated waymark post on the right. At the right-hand end of the middle plantation is a gate.

4 Go through the gate and turn right through another gate. Follow a vague path alongside a low ridge, with rocky outcrops on your left. On some of those you will find good examples of cup and ring markings. Ahead of you is a patch of gorse and a few trees hiding a signpost and a kissing gate which takes you onto a road. Turn right and walk along the road passing the entrance to **Fowberry Moor Farm** on the left. The road turns in here but keep on along a track. On the right are a trig point and the **Repeater Relay Station**. Just beyond is a gate on the left.

5 Go through the gate and follow a grassy track which bears round a plantation and arrives at a T-junction. Turn right and follow the edge of the woodland on the right. The **Coldmartin Loughs** are hidden in the woodland. Pass the **Repeater Station** on your right and join a road. Walk down this road – there is a good view over **Wooler** – and descend to the signpost which originally led you up to **Weetwood Moor** and thence back into **Brewery Lane**. Retrace your steps to the **Tankerville Arms**.

Places of interest nearby

Ford and Etal villages lie close together, just off the A697, about 8 miles north of Wooler. Take a right turn just after Milfield along the B6353 and follow the signs. Amongst the many attractions are a working corn mill, a narrow gauge light railway, Etal Castle (English Heritage) and the Lady Waterford Hall in Ford decorated with life-size paintings of biblical scenes by the Marchioness of Waterford, who used local children and adults as models for the characters. There is also Ford Nursery in the walled garden of Ford Castle, and the Horseshoe Forge Pottery. As if all of that was not enough, there is Ford Moss Nature Reserve.
☎ 01890 820338; website: www.ford-and-etal.co.uk

The Ship

Nowadays **the icon** of Northumbrian tourism, Holy Island, or Lindisfarne, was one of the main centres of Christianity in the Dark Ages. It was the home of the charismatic St Cuthbert of whom there are numerous reminders. The castle which dominates the island from its curious basalt outcrop was built with stones from the ruined priory – its most exciting moment, though, was when it was captured by two enterprising Jacobites in 1715. The island is part of the Lindisfarne Nature Reserve which is notable for a wide variety of birds and wildfowl, as well as wild flowers, including orchids and hellebores. Of course, the famous Lindisfarne mead is also made commercially on the island. This is a lovely walk on grassy paths and along a very picturesque enclosed 'lonnen'.

Distance – 4 miles or 3 miles.

OS Explorer 340 Holy Island and Bamburgh. GR 124417. An easy walk with no inclines. The route follows tracks and sandy and grassy paths.

Starting point The Ship on Holy Island.

How to get there Holy Island is 6 miles east of the A1 across a 3-mile causeway. Turn off the A1 at Beal. However, it must be noted that since the causeway to Holy Island is tidal, it can be reached only at low tide. Tide tables are available from Tourist Information Centres (there is a good one in Alnwick), and from Northumberland County Council (www.northumberland.gov. uk/vg/holyisland, telephone 01665 577285). Tide times are also published in local newspapers. Parking is restricted to residents but there is a large pay-and-display car park on the edge of the village.

THE PUB The **Ship** (known locally as The Tavern) is a whitewashed inn set in a terraced row. It has the atmosphere of a small wooden ship. Beers available are Theakston's, John Smith's, Exmoor Gold, Holy Island Blessed Bitter and Secret Kingdom. There is an extensive range of food on offer. There are light lunches, sandwich specials (including the local crab and prawns) and a special children's menu. Main courses include fresh local fish dishes such as lobster tails and its famous fish and chips

and home-made steak and stout pie. The prices are reasonable.
There is a pleasant beer garden. Accommodation is available.

*Open from 12 pm to 3 pm and then 6 pm to 11 pm. Food is
available from 12 pm to 2 pm and 6 pm to 7.30 pm.*
☎ *01289 389311; website: www.theshipinn-holyisland.co.uk*

1 From the **Ship**, turn left and then left again into **Sandham Lane**.
Now follow this lane beside the old curing house and coastguard
cottages to **Coombs Farm**. It reduces into a very pleasant farm
track. Stay on this, the **Straight Lonnen**. Go through a wicket
gate into a National Nature Reserve.

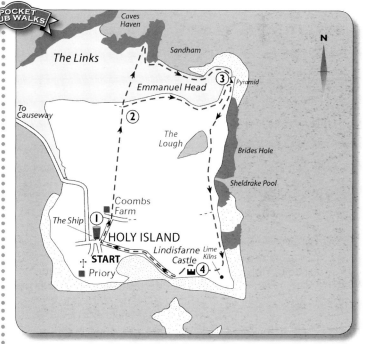

Lindisfarne Castle on Holy Island.

2 Here you have two options. *For the shorter route*, turn right and go along a clear track with a wall more or less close to the right until you approach a large white pyramid (a navigation aid) over to the left. From the corner of the wall, take a path bearing left to this and continue from point 3 below. *Alternatively, for the full walk*, from the wicket gate bear left and follow a path marked with white-tipped stakes which will take you over the old golf links and to the sandstone cliffs of **Coves Haven** and the very pretty **Sandham Bay**. From here you can simply retrace your steps and take the route from the signboard given above, or you could follow a path by the edge of **Sandham Bay** towards the gleaming pyramid.

3 From **Emmanuel Head** and the pyramid, bear round to the right on a grassy path southwards for about 1 mile. The castle is soon in view and is your next target. You approach the wall which marks the boundary of the **National Nature Reserve**. Keep on for a few yards until you cross a stile to the right. Turn

left and continue. Stay away from the edge of the low cliff. Go through a kissing gate and continue along an open grassy track, passing **Brides Hole** on the left and **Holy Island Lough** on the right. The path bears right to meet a fence. You pass a public footpath sign and track on the right. Continue with the fence to your right and a rocky beach to the left, through a gate and then along a raised track towards **Lindisfarne Castle** and three upturned coble hulls beside **Castle Point**, reminders of the once sizeable fishing fleet of the island.

4 Cross a footbridge and pass to the right of the castle to join the road into the village. Alternatively you could continue on to the thin stretch of beach (**The Stank**) where you can walk between the water's edge and upturned cobles and past old herring houses to a jetty. Bear right from here to rise to a ridge called the **Heugh**. Pass through a swing-gate and walk by the priory wall past the **Crown and Anchor** to the village green.

Places of interest nearby

Lindisfarne Priory (English Heritage) has been a place of pilgrimage since the corpse of St Cuthbert was found here, undecayed, 11 years after his death in AD 687.
☎ 01289 389200

The **Lindisfarne Centre** (English Heritage) tells the story of Holy Island.
☎ 01289 389004

Lindisfarne Castle (National Trust) was converted into a private house in 1903 by Edwin Lutyens for Edward Hudson, founder of *Country Life*. The small rooms are full of intimate decorations and design, with windows looking down upon the walled garden planned by Gertrude Jekyll.
☎ 01289 389244; website: www.nationaltrust.org.uk

The Masons Arms

he striking ruin of Norham Castle, its pink sandstone set against dark green trees, was a popular subject for the painter, Turner. Built in 1158 it guarded a key ford over the Tweed. For many years, Norhamshire was an enclave belonging to the Bishop of Durham and not part of Northumberland, which explains the grandeur of St Cuthbert's church. Edward I declared himself Paramount King of Scotland here. The castle was involved in numerous sieges and campaigns, and figures in the poem *Marmion* by Sir Walter Scott. Now peaceful, Norham has the appearance and feel of a Scottish village. The outward route follows riverside paths and the edge of Newbiggin Dene. The return to Norham is via a short stretch on a very quiet country lane and paths along field edges.

THE PUB The **Masons Arms** is a small local, with genuine character. Many of the decorations, inevitably, are fishing rods. There is a real fire in the small and intimate public bar and the beers are Belhaven and Deuchars. Occasionally there are the shouts of a noisy cockatoo in the background. You can eat either at the bar or in the small restaurant. There is a range of excellent home-made soups ('a meal in itself', as they are advertised). Main courses include substantial home-made choices such as Mick's grill, sausage and liver casserole and honey roast pork. Food is all fresh (or to put it more directly, 'Oh no, we never have anything lying about...'). There is also a range of sandwiches and a small sweets menu. Children are very welcome. Dogs are allowed in the bar.

Open from 11 am to 11 pm. Food is served from 12 pm to 2 pm and from 7 pm to 8.30 pm. No food is served on Sunday evenings.
☎ *01289 382326*

Distance – 4½ miles.

OS Explorer 339 Kelso, Coldstream and the Lower Tweed Valley. GR 902474.
One short uphill section but otherwise level. Some walking on a quiet road.

Starting point The Masons Arms in Norham.

How to get there Turn off the A698 between Berwick-on-Tweed and Cornhill-on-Tweed onto the B6470, which will take you into Norham. The Masons Arms stands near the village green and you can park easily by the roadside.

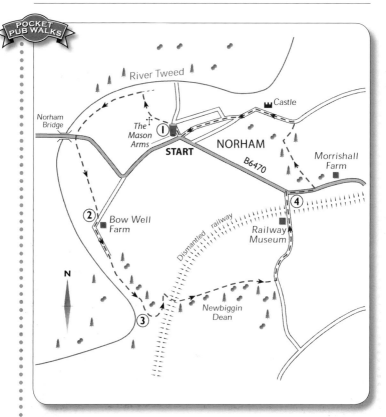

POCKET PUB WALKS

River Tweed

Norham Bridge

The Mason Arms ① START

Castle

NORHAM

B6470

Morrishall Farm

② Bow Well Farm

Dismantled railway

Railway Museum

④

N

③

Newbiggin Dean

1 Turn left out of the **Masons Arms** and walk to the village green. Turn left there and walk along **Pedwell Way**, past a sign to **Ladykirk Bridge** and **Twizell Bridge** and on to **St Cuthbert's church**. Enter the graveyard by a double gate (signed **The Tweed**). Walk through the churchyard on a grassy path between gravestones, passing behind the north side of the church. To the right of a sign 'No Public Right of Way', enter an enclosed path down to the **Tweed**. Turn left and follow the river upstream to **Ladykirk** and **Norham Bridge**. Continue on the same side of

the river through a kissing gate and then beneath the bridge and cross a stile on your left.

2. Turn right over the stile and walk along the field edge. As you approach **Bow Well Farm**, cross a stile to the right, then follow the path down a wooded bank and out through a wicket gate onto a lane. Turn right and when the lane ends, pass through a wicket gate (signed **Twizell Bridge**) and continue over pastureland in front of a cottage (past a couple of thoughtful stone nymphs) and then through a field gate into a wood. The path continues by the river. You reach a junction of paths and a footbridge to the right.

3. At the path junction, go left through a broken gate. Bear left (waymarked) beyond this and climb up steps to another junction at the top of the wood. Turn right and walk along **Newbiggin Dean**, beneath a railway viaduct. Cross a stile (signed back to

Norham Castle.

West Newbiggin) and at a path junction take the right fork (signed **East Newbiggin**) which leads, high above woods, to a lane. At the lane, turn left and walk on, past the former **Norham station** (now a private railway museum with limited opening hours) and between the piers of the old railway bridge.

4 At the junction of the lane with the B6470, turn right and then soon turn left through an opening onto a bridleway (signed **Norham Castle**). Cross a footbridge and go through a wicket gate and then follow the left-hand edge of the field to the left corner with a brook to your left. Go through a wicket gate into a wood. Continue on to cross a bridge to the left into a field. In the field, turn right and follow the edge of the field to exit by a field gate (signed back to **Morrishall Farm**) in a lane. Turn left here and walk past the entrance of **Norham Castle** and then down the bank back into **Norham**.

Places of interest nearby

Norham Castle (English Heritage) is open at the weekends and bank holidays between April and September.
☎ 01289 382329

If romantic ruins aren't your scene, visit the **Chain Bridge Honey Farm**. Here you will find a honey and beekeeping museum, an observation hive, marvellous murals, a vintage vehicle collection and unique café in a restored vintage double-decker bus. You can buy beeswax products and – of course – loads of honey. It stands near the famous Union Chain Bridge, which was completed in 1820 and is the oldest suspension bridge in Britain still open to traffic. The Chain Bridge Honey Farm is accessible from the A698 Berwick to Coldstream road a mile from the A1, or from the A1 East Ord roundabout. Costs nothing for admission!
☎ 01289 386362; website: www.chainbridgehoney.co.uk